More favourite walks around Oswestry and the Borders

ramblers
at the heart of walking

Oswestry Group of the Ramblers

First Published 2011 by Shropshire Area Ramblers

© Oswestry Group of the Ramblers
Tre Tylluan, Dolybont, Llanrhaeadr Ym Mochnant, Oswestry SY10 0LJ

ISBN 9780-9569021-0-8

Design, maps and production by Jane and Ray Hadlow

Edited by Peter Carr

Cover photographs of Old Oswestry Hillfort by Ray Hadlow

Typeset in Minion and Frutiger

Printed by WPG Ltd, Welshpool

Great care has been taken in the compilation of this publication to ensure
accuracy. However, the publishers cannot accept responsibility for any errors
that may appear, changes post publication to the footpaths used, or the
consequences of errors or changes. If you are in any doubt about access, check
before you proceed.

The Oswestry Group acknowledges with grateful thanks the efforts of all
members who have checked, walked and re-checked these walks to ensure that
they are as accurate as possible.

The Ramblers' Association is a company limited by guarantee, registered in
England and Wales. Company registration number: 4458492. Registered Charity
in England and Wales number 1093577, registered charity number in Scotland,
number SC039799.

Registered Office: 2nd floor, Camelford House, 87-90 Albert Embankment,
London SE1 7TW

Introduction

When we published our first volume of walks 'Favourite Walks around Oswestry and the Borders' little did we realise just how popular it was going to be. It was received with enthusiasm by both visitors and residents to the extent that we had sold out in six months. We have been faced with constant requests to publish a second book of similar walks; the result is this new book.

Covering the same range of countryside as book 1, this book has sixteen walks which will introduce users to the very varied countryside we have on our doorstep.

The walks in the Tanat Valley, while relatively strenuous, provide spectacular views of the Berwyn Mountains, the Tanat Valley and the Shropshire Plain. The walks down in the south introduce the countryside around the confluence of the Rivers Severn and Vyrnwy. We have included four walks of different lengths and grades from Oswestry town centre to introduce the lovely countryside literally on the doorstep. In the north we have two walks in the lovely but steep sided Ceiriog Valley and over to the east we introduce walkers to Overton and the river Dee.

We love to walk in this area of unspoilt countryside, and are pleased to introduce it to you and believe that you will come to enjoy it as we do. Nothing pleases us more than to meet people on our walks enjoying this area we call our Oswestry Ramblers' area for the first time.

Good walking

Peter Carr
Editor and Chairman of the Oswestry Group of Ramblers

Location of walks

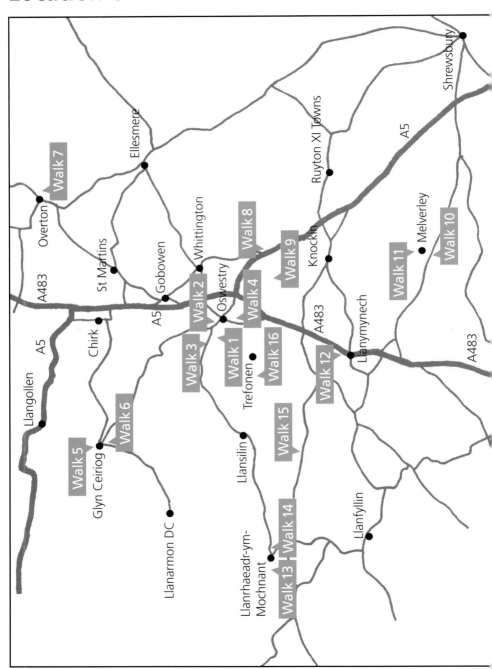

Summary of walks

Walk Number	Brief Description	Start Point & Grid Ref	Distance (Approx)	Grade
1 (page 1)	Oswald's Well and Offa's Dyke	Cae Glas Park in Oswestry – SJ 289294	5.9 miles	Moderate
2 (page 4)	Oswestry to Hengoed and back	Gatacre CP, Oswestry – SJ 324368	3.75 miles	Leisurely
3 (page 7)	A circular walk from Oswestry including Brogyntyn Park	Central CP, Oswestry – SJ 291295	6.2 miles	Leisurely
4 (page 9)	Oswestry to Morda and back through Broomhall	Central CP, Oswestry – SJ 291295	3.8 miles	Leisurely
5 (page 11)	A short walk from Glyn Ceiriog – river and hill	The Cross in Glyn Ceiriog – SJ 202378	3.1 miles	Moderate
6 (page 14)	The Glyn Valley Tramway and Llwybr Ceiriog Trail	The Cross in Glyn Ceiriog – SJ 202378	5.5 miles	Moderate
7 (page 16)	A circuit from Overton	Overton, behind St Mary's Church – SJ 374418	5.6 miles	Leisurely
8 (page 19)	Queen's Head and Montgomery Canal	CP opposite the Queen's Head – SJ 339268	4.25 miles	Leisurely
9 (page 21)	The 'Monty' – Maesbury Marsh, Crickheath and Morton	Canal Central café, Maesbury Marsh – SJ 310249	4.6 miles	Leisurely
10 (page 24)	Bausley Hill and the River Severn	Layby at Melverley Bridge – SJ 331158	4.8 miles	Moderate
11 (page 26)	A stroll around Melverley	Layby at Melverley Bridge – SJ 331158	5.6 miles	Leisurely
12 (page 28)	Blodwel Rock and Llanymynech Quarry	CP at end of Underhill Lane, Pant – SJ 271219	3.7 miles	Leisurely
13 (page 31)	Llanarmon Mynydd Mawr	CP in Llanrhaeadr Ym Mochnant – SJ 125261	5.5 miles	Moderate
14 (page 34)	Moel Hen-fache circuit	CP in Llanrhaeadr Ym Mochnant – SJ 125261	5.9 miles	Moderate
15 (page 37)	Llangedwyn and Briw	CP at Craft Centre, Llangedwyn – SJ 185241	5.4 miles	Moderate
16 (page 40)	Trefonen to Craig Sychtyn Nature Reserve and back via the Mynydd Myfyr	Chapel Green CP, Trefonen – SJ 260267	6 miles	Moderate

Walk Grades

- **Leisurely Walks** for reasonably fit people with at least a little country walking experience. May include unsurfaced rural paths and fields. Walking boots and warm, waterproof clothing are recommended.
- **Moderate Walks** for people with country walking experience and a good level of fitness. May include some steep paths and open country. Walking boots and warm, waterproof clothing are essential.
- **Strenuous Walks** for experienced country walkers with an above average fitness level. May include hills and rough country. Walking boots and warm, waterproof clothing are essential.

Maps

Note: maps are sketches only and are not necessarily to scale

The Countryside code

- Be safe – plan ahead and follow any signs
- Leave gates and property as you find them
- Protect plants and animals, and take your litter home
- Keep dogs under close control
- Consider other people

Useful Information

Footpath problems in Shropshire
Contact Countryside Service – Shropshire Council
Tel: 01743 255061
Email: countryside.access@shropshire.gov.uk

Footpath problems in the Ceiriog Valley
Contact the Rights of Way and Access Team – Wrexham County Borough Council
Tel: 01978 292057
Email: rightsofway@wrexham.gov.uk

Footpath problems in Powys
Contact Countryside Services – Powys County Council
Tel: 01597 827500
Email: rightsofway@powys.gov.uk

Buses from Oswestry
Traveline West Midlands Tel: 0871 200 22 33
www.travelinemidlands.co.uk

The Ramblers
Membership and any other enquiries:
2nd floor, Camelford House, 87-90 Albert Embankment, London SE1 7TW
Tel: 020 7339 8500
www.ramblers.org.uk

Oswald's Well and Offa's Dyke

Chris Jenkins

GRADE	Moderate
MAP	OS Explorer™ Sheet 240
START POINT	Cae Glas Park in Church Street, Oswestry – Grid Ref SJ 289294
DISTANCE	5.9 miles (9.5 km)
TOTAL ASCENT	700 ft (213 m) approx
DURATION	3.25 hours
TERRAIN	Good paths, fields and woods

This walk leaves Oswestry and goes to the west of the town via Oswald's Well then over fields via the remains of the walled gardens of Llanforda Hall to the Offa's Dyke Path. Then climbs up through woods and returns to Oswestry via fields and lanes. Good views of the Shropshire Plain are afforded.

Legend has it that after the Battle of Maserfield (642 AD) an eagle carried the severed arm of the defeated Oswald of Northumbria to the location of Oswald's Well and a spring then appeared. Though the Christian Oswald was defeated by the pagan Penda of Mercia, Oswald is remembered as a saint and the name Oswestry derives from 'Oswald's Tree' (in Welsh Croes Oswallt literally Oswald's Cross).

During the walk, the ruins and the walled garden, all that is left of Llanforda Hall, will be encountered. This was home of the Lloyd family from the seventeenth century, and associated with the naturalist Edward Lhuyd. There were once extensive gardens and parklands around the hall. The last of several buildings on the site was demolished in 1949.

Offa's Dyke, which is crossed by the walk, is an earthworks embankment which is thought to have been a political boundary between Saxon Mercia and Wales built during the reign of King Offa of Mercia (757-796 AD). The Offa's Dyke Path runs for 177 miles from Sedbury Cliffs on the Severn Estuary near Chepstow to the North Wales resort of Prestatyn on Liverpool Bay. For about 70 miles it follows the course of the Offa's Dyke earthwork.

DIRECTIONS

1 Starting from the gates of Cae Glas Park in Church Street, go past the artillery memorial and across to the opposite side of the park and into Welsh Walls. Cross the road (carefully) and turn left in front of the Walls restaurant, cross Brynhafod Road and enter the playing field. The row of trees on the right are a war memorial to ex-pupils from the old Grammar School (now the Magistrates Court) on the left. Walk across the field to a gate on the left-hand side beyond the buildings. Turn right and on the left side of the road look out for Oswald's Well (see notes above). Continue up Maserfield Road and bear left along a

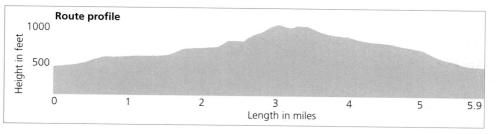

Route profile

Height in feet — Length in miles

tree-lined road to an iron gate into Broomhall Lane (GR 281290).

2 Turn right just past Rose Cottage then take a stile on the left into a field. The next stile is a little way right of the far corner of this field. Be careful crossing a damp area below a spring. Over the stile go forward and slightly left to join a track leading to a gate and stile. Cross the road to a ladder stile and follow the track beyond leading up to a patch of woodland. Cross a stile into the wood and go forward about 70 m to a junction of paths (GR 266290).

3 Take the path to the left above a bank with a show of snowdrops in season to a stile and cross a field to a gate and stile. Look back on the right to see the walled garden of Llanforda Hall (see notes above). Go forward just left of some trees and look for a square of fencing protecting a tree

with two waymarks – follow the right-hand path to a gate at the back of Keeper's Cottage. In a few yards bear right up a slope into the woods and forward to an area with young trees and slightly right to join a track. Go left then right at a junction and then left by a marker post to the right. You then join the Offa's Dyke Path coming up from the Candy Brook. (The Offa's Dyke Path is a long distance path signposted with an acorn throughout its length) (GR 255286).

4 Turn right to follow the Offa's Dyke Path below the dyke until it passes back over the dyke, through an old stone wall to the English side. Here leave the Offa's Dyke Path and continue ahead down a track to Bwlch (GR 257297).

5 Go straight along a minor road, round a corner to the left and forward to a

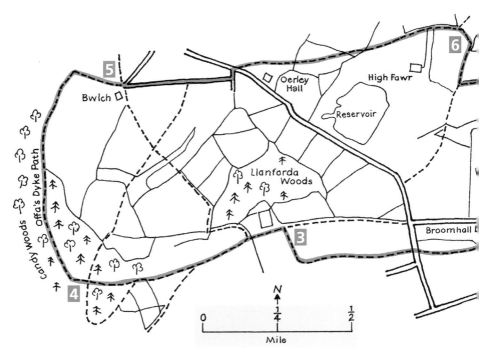

road junction. Cross the road to a gate and take the right-hand path to a projecting hedge corner and then continuing to a gate near the opposite corner of the field. Go through the gate and look for a water trough in the hedge on the right, cross at this point into the next field. Go diagonally across this field to another stile then follow the hedge on the left crossing two more stiles (ignoring a path on the left). Follow the hedge round the field to the right, over two more stiles then go left through a gate into a green lane (GR 276298).

6 Follow the lane downhill crossing other roads until it becomes tarmac and then joins Brynhafod Road. Continue down until you find a gate on the right into the playing field crossed at the start of the walk and then return to the start of the walk via the outward route.

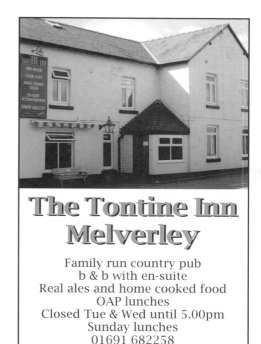

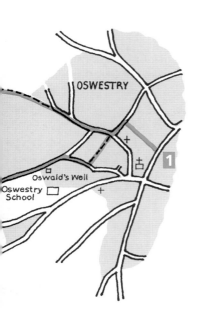

OSWESTRY

Oswald's Well

Oswestry
School

1

Photo: New bridge by Cross Lanes farm, see Walk 2 / Ray Hadlow

Oswestry to Hengoed and back

Jane Hadlow

2

Grade	Leisurely
Map	OS Explorer™ Sheet 240
Start point	Gatacre car park – Grid Ref SJ 291305
Distance	3.75 miles (6 km)
Total ascent	275 ft (84 m) approx
Duration	2 hours
Terrain	Field paths and quiet lanes with a short gentle climb. The walk can be quite muddy in places

This is a gentle walk across fields of crops and grass with a bit of lane walking and includes part of Wat's Dyke and passes Old Oswestry Hillfort.

Old Oswestry Hillfort is one of the best preserved hillforts in Britain. This very impressive Iron Age hillfort covers 40 acres and has multiple ramparts built at different times. People used the hillfort from the Neolithic through to Roman times but mostly from 1000BC (before any ramparts were built) to AD43.

After the hillfort fell into disuse it became incorporated into Wat's Dyke. This is a linear earthwork of 40 miles running parallel to Offa's Dyke but built at an earlier date. This runs along the border between the Welsh hills and the Shropshire/Cheshire lowlands.

Directions

1 Leave the car park at the top left-hand corner and after 20 m cross a stile. From the stile walk to the field edge and follow the hedge on the left until it turns away to the left. At this point keep straight on across the open field to a stile in the corner. Cross the stile through the hedge and carry straight on across two more fields and stiles. After the second stile head to the left of the highest point of the hill to a gate with a stile beside it. Cross the stile and go straight down following the fence on the right to a stile onto a track (GR 289319).

2 Turn left along on the track for 80 m passing a house on the right and cross the stile (iron bars in a wall) on the right into a short enclosed path. Cross the next stile and turn right to follow the hedge on the right until it drops away to the right, then carry straight on across the field to a stile. Go right, through a gate on the right. Turn left and cross the open field to a kink in the hedge on the left. Follow the hedge to the far corner where there is a stream and a new bridge. Cross the bridge into the next field (GR 291324).

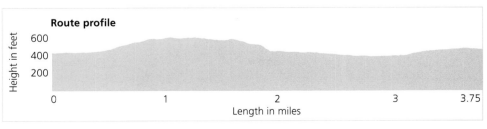

Route profile

3 Carry straight on across the field to cross a stile and head for the electicity power pole, half left from the gate. A hedge (more a clump of thorns) appears on the left – keep to the right of this to a stile in the hedge ahead and onto the lane. Turn left along the lane to the crossroads. Turn right and walk 300 m down the lane to a gate on the right just past Brymeg Cottage, standing alone (GR 295328).

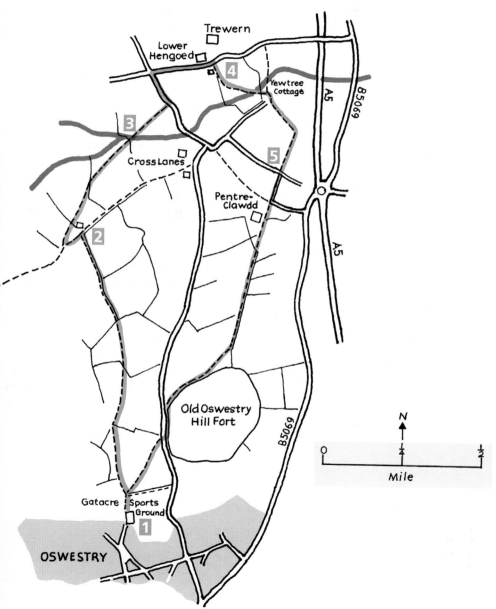

4 Go through the gate and follow the house fence and then the hedge for 50 m and then go diagonally across to the far left-hand corner. Cross the stile and then in a few metres, turn right across a footbridge to emerge by Yewtree Cottage. Keep the house on your left as you pass onto the track and then cross over the stile on the left into the field. Head across the field to a few standing trees in the middle and carry on to meet the fence on the opposite side. This is the line of Wat's Dyke. Turn right to follow this hedge line through the gate and along the edge of the next field to a stile onto a lane (GR 299323).

5 Go straight ahead along the lane to Pentre Clawdd farmhouse. Go over the stile to the left of the entrance wall, into the field. Follow the wall on the right, then the hedge and where it turns to the right continue on to a gate and stile. Go over the stile and then head straight on with the hedge on the left (Wat's Dyke again). Keep the hedge on your left as the Hillfort now looms ahead. Cross another stile into the next field. The path continues along the hedge line for another 150 m and then crosses diagonally to the far right-hand corner, through a gate into the lane. Turn left along the lane to the entrance to the Hillfort (there are good views from the top!). Go through the gap in the hedge opposite the entrance and follow the path diagonally across the field to a kissing gate in the far corner which joins the outward path.

Brogyntyn Park

Clive La-Garde

GRADE	Leisurely
MAP	OS Explorer™ Sheet 240
START POINT	Central car park, Oswestry – Grid Ref SJ 291295
DISTANCE	6.2 miles (10 km)
TOTAL ASCENT	550 ft (167 m) approx
DURATION	3.5 hours
TERRAIN	Lanes, tracks, fields and roads (2.25 miles of this walk is on lanes and roads)

Brogyntyn or Porkington as it was sometimes called is built on the site of the medieval hall of Madog ap Maredudd, the last king of Powys. The original Castell Brogyntyn was sited about 400 m north west of the present hall. Owain Brogyntyn, illegitimate son of Maddog succeeded him as prince of Lower Powys plus various other lordships. He was a very distinguished leader and was responsible for the defeat of the English at the Battle of Grogen in 1165. Brogyntyn is one of the few Shropshire estates surviving from the middle ages.

The pedigree of the Ormsby-Gore family goes back to 1559, when Robert ap John married Gwenhwyfar, daughter of William ap Meredith ap Rhys. Members of the family have been prominent in public life as MPs for Irish constituencies and later for North Shropshire. The estate has been continuously occupied for eight hundred and fifty years through to the middle of the 20th century.

DIRECTIONS

1 Leave from top right corner of the car park on to the road 'English Walls' and go right to mini roundabout and then left into Leg Street to the traffic lights, cross over and follow the road around into Beatrice Street and continue on through traffic lights to Gitten Street opposite Morrison's supermarket. Walk up Gitten Street, over two crossroads, passing a junior school on the right to the junction with Gatacre Road, bear right to the sport's centre parking area at 100 m (GR 291305).

2 With the hedge on the left walk up 50 m to find a gap in the hedge, go left through the gap and follow the path to a kissing gate into a field. Ignore the path on the right; keep the hedge on the left for 150 m, then go ahead to the corner of the field to a hidden stile. Cross this stile and the next at 100 m, walk up the hill to a gate and on down the field, keeping the fence to the right, up to a gate/stile on to a track. Turn left on the track and walk down to the B4579 – Oswestry to Selattyn road (GR 283316).

3 Cross the road half left to a gate leading into Brogyntyn Park and follow the road passing the main building on the left. The road continues past the

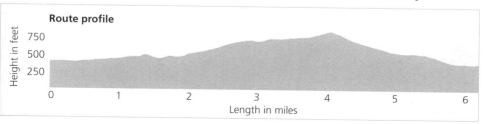

Route profile

Height in feet / Length in miles

stables and through the walled garden area into open parkland through an avenue of trees eventually arriving at the home farm. Continue on the track to reach a minor road where you take a left turn and walk to the B4580 – Oswestry to the Racecourse road (GR 269308).

4 Cross the road onto a track, passing houses on the left to a gate. There are two further gates. After the second of these gates take the footpath on the left, through the gate and walk half right towards the corner of a small copse. Continue to a stile in a hedge approximately 50 m from the right-hand fence line and follow the fence line ahead crossing two further stiles to reach a minor road (GR 263298).

5 Turn left on this road and walk down for 1.5 km passing Oerley Hall on the left, also on the left a reservoir presumably connected to the water works further down

the road. Ignore the footpath on the left just after the bend and continue past the junction with Broomhall Lane to find a footpath on the left (GR 274289).

6 Take this path for 200 m, then bear left to a corner of a fence on your right. (There may or not be a stile here, the hedge has recently been cut down). Continue along the fence line to a stile onto Broomhall Lane. Turn right and go down Broomhall Lane to a T junction, turn left and go down the road to the traffic lights. Turn left into the town to a mini-roundabout, then turn right and go diagonally across the square to the main car park to finish.

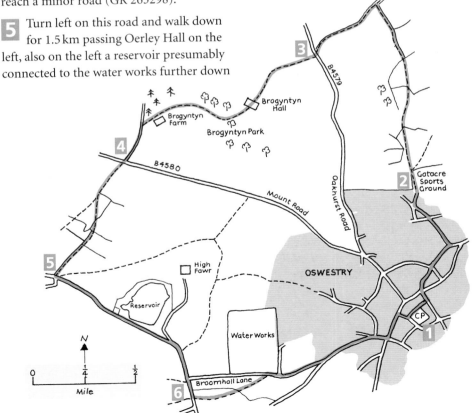

Oswestry to Morda and back through Broomhall

Clive La-Garde

Grade	Leisurely
Map	OS Explorer™ Sheet 240
Start point	Central car park, Oswestry Grid Ref SJ 291295
Distance	3.8 miles (6.1 km)
Total ascent	260 ft (80 m) approx
Duration	2 hours
Terrain	Lanes, tracks, fields and roads

This walk starts at the Central car park in Oswestry, goes past the town cemetery to Weston Lane, then turns west towards Morda, once an area of coal mining and brick works. From Morda the walk turns north towards Llanforda then east towards Broomhall and Oswestry. As you leave Love Lane, ahead you will see Penylan Mill. The mill was built for grinding corn and in the 1860's a boiler and chimney were added, but these were never used because imported grain was then being processed at the port of entry. The mill is now a private residence.

Directions

1 From the Central car park in Oswestry, take the vehicle exit into Roft Street and continue straight ahead from the car park exit. At the junction with Victoria Road, turn left in and 200 m the take

the 2nd turn right into Queens Road. Go along Queens Road for 25 m, then go through the kissing gate on the left to a footpath running parallel to a new housing development. At the bottom of the footpath, go through a kissing gate into a field and turn right to walk along the field edge. At the end of the field, turn left to take a footpath between a hedge and the cemetery fence (this path can be muddy in wet weather). At the end of the path, go right through a kissing gate and across the field to another kissing gate. Go through the gate and slightly left down to, and through, another kissing gate into an enclosed path. Go along the path and where another path comes in from the left via a kissing gate, bear right to continue along the enclosed path for 400 m to a further kissing gate onto Weston Lane (GR 294282).

2 Turn right and in just a few metres, take the stile on the left into a field. Head down to the bottom of the field and the edge of a stream. Go through the hedge line and head to the right of the buildings just ahead. Go through the gate and turn right onto a wide track (leads to a small

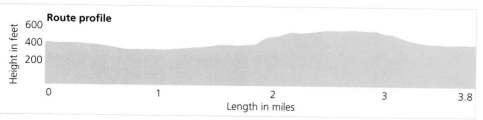

Route profile

Height in feet — 600, 400, 200

Length in miles — 0, 1, 2, 3, 3.8

industrial site just to the left). Go along the track to the Morda Road (B5096). Cross the road to a stile opposite and go up a wide track, passing a house, and go straight ahead to a stile. Cross the stile into Love Lane. Turn left and continue on to a junction with a road. Turn left along the road and in 100 m, just as the road swings left, take the stile on the right into a field (GR 281282).

3 Go up the field to a stile onto Penylan Lane. Turn left and continue to a stile on the right, just past the house on the right. Go diagonally left across the field to a gate in the middle of the hedge, then continue diagonally left to a stile onto the Oswestry–Trefonen Road. Taking care,

cross the road to the pavement opposite, turn left and in 20 m, turn right into a minor road (GR 275285).

4 Continue along the road for 350 m and at a footpath crossing, take the stile on the right. Go along the path for 200 m, then bear left to a corner of a fence on your right. (There may or not be a stile here, the hedge has recently been cut down). Continue along to the left of the fence line to a stile onto Broomhall Lane. Turn right and go down Broomhall Lane to a T junction, turn left and go down the road to the traffic lights. Turn left into the town to a mini-roundabout, then turn right and go diagonally across the square to the main car park to finish.

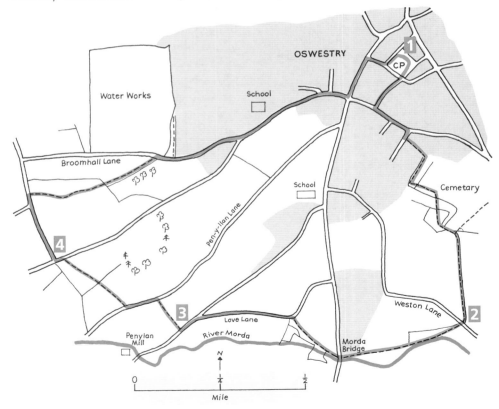

Glyn Ceiriog – river and hill

George Swift

GRADE	Moderate
MAP	OS Explorer™ Sheet 255
START POINT	The Cross in Glyn Ceiriog – Grid Ref SJ 202378. Parking in Glyn Ceiriog is limited. There is a small car park at the back of the Glyn Valley Hotel. If this is full, park sensibly on the road
DISTANCE	3.1 miles (5 km)
TOTAL ASCENT	860 ft (263 m) approx
DURATION	2 hours
TERRAIN	Lanes, tracks, fields and roads – steep in places

'A little bit of heaven on Earth' was how Lloyd George described the Ceiriog Valley. This beautiful valley has remained relatively undiscovered. Only a few miles from the busy A5, it has retained its cultural heritage and lovely countryside. However, much of the now idyllic Ceiriog Valley was once a grim, grey place, with industries based on its rock and mineral deposits. All around Glyn Ceiriog was a bleak landscape of spoil heaps. In 1873 a narrow gauge railway was built, the mineral industry created the tramway and because the tramway existed it in turn gave birth to other industries – from out of the valley came slate and over the years were added granite, china stone, tar macadam and even gunpowder. From the mills came cloth and from the valley's trout fishery live trout; a passenger service was also added. The last train ran through the valley in 1935 – the news had gone round, and scores of locals turned out at Glyn to see the 'tram' go by, never to return. There is now an active tramway preservation society that aims to re-open at least part of the tramway.

Attractive woodland, achieved by a combination of sensitive planting and natural regeneration, have almost eliminated the scars left by industry. Had Lloyd George not spoken so passionately in its defence, we may never have known of the beauty of the Ceiriog Valley; in 1923 Parliament was asked to grant statutory powers to impound the upper waters of the River Ceiriog and to evict the local population living within an area of 13,600 acres. With such an eloquent advocate, the proposal was defeated.

DIRECTIONS

1 From the Village Cross take the B4579 Selattyn Road and walk past the Post Office which will be on the right. Follow the road around to the right and across the bridge over the River Ceiriog. After crossing the bridge turn immediately right up a lane, the river is to the right. Go 100 m up the lane to the Upper Mills Trout Farm down on the right. After the Trout Farm the lane climbs steadily and then quite steeply. After approximately 1 mile you will

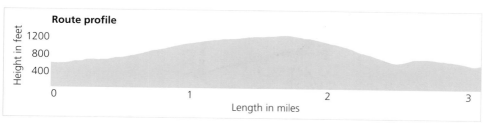

Route profile

Height in feet — 1200, 800, 400

Length in miles — 0, 1, 2, 3

arrive at Pant Farm on the left hand side (GR 205365).

2 Immediately after Pant Farm, bear left along a track. After about 500 m you will reach some farm buildings (GR 210364).

3 Go over the stile immediately on the left before the farm buildings (this stile is not visible until you are right up to it). Follow the hedge line up the field and through a gate to another stile. Cross this stile and bear left up the footpath to reach the fence on the right. Follow this fence line to arrive at another stile in some gorse

bushes (GR 207366). *Before reaching this stile, sit and rest a while and enjoy the view of the beautiful Ceiriog Valley.*

4 After crossing the stile turn right through some gorse bushes and head for the waymarker post. After the waymarker post bear slightly left to another waymarker post and then head for the gap in a low stone wall. Carry straight on down the field to the far corner near some pine trees (GR 206370). *From this corner you can look down onto the Trout Farm that you passed earlier.*

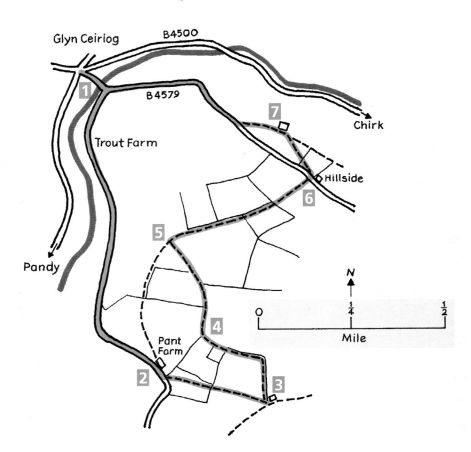

5 Head east following a stone wall and gorse bushes for about 150 m to arrive at a waymarker post on the left with waymarkers pointing in all directions! Go straight on here down a clearly defined track and keep to the left at the 'Y' junction. Carry on down between the line of trees and over the stile into a field then straight on keeping the fence to the right. The path a little further on is slippery in the wet and is very stony underfoot – walk this section with great care! Cross over the stile on the right and turn immediately left and over another stile in front of you. Go down the stone steps and turn left passing in front of the bungalow and step down onto the road, the B4579 (GR 212373).

6 Go straight across this road and down some steps by the side of a house called Hillside. Turn left at the bottom of the steps and go over the stile. Carry straight on and follow the path along the side of the field until you arrive at a Pony Trekking Centre (GR 211375).

7 Go straight ahead here up a steep lane keeping the buildings on the right to reach the B4579. Turn right and walk back down into the village of Glyn Ceiriog and return to the start of the walk.

Glyn Valley Tramway and Llwybr Ceiriog Trail

George Swift

GRADE	Moderate
MAP	OS Explorer™ Sheet 255
START POINT	The Cross in Glyn Ceiriog – Grid Ref SJ 202378. Parking in Glyn Ceiriog is limited. There is a small car park at the back of the Glyn Valley Hotel. If this is full, park sensibly on the road.
DISTANCE	5.5 miles (8.85 km)
TOTAL ASCENT	1110 ft (338 m) approx
DURATION	3.25 hours
TERRAIN	Minor roads, lanes and disused tramway

This walk takes in part of the Glyn Valley Tramway route (see walk 5 – page 11) and part of the Llwybr Ceiriog Trail. The Llwybr Ceiriog Trail is a circular route of about 18 miles based on Llanarmon Dyffryn Ceiriog which passes to the west of Pandy, it was developed primarily for horse riders, but the part included in this walk is equally suitable for walkers and provides stunning views of the Ceiriog Valley.

DIRECTIONS

1 From Glyn Ceiriog walk south along the B4500 keeping the Glyn Valley Hotel on the right and passing a public toilet on the left. Continue for approximately 0.8 miles (1.29 km) to arrive at Ddol Hir Caravan Park on the left-hand side. Keep on the main road past the caravan park and up a slight incline to a National Trust sign on the left saying 'Glyn Valley Tramway' (GR 199364).

2 Go through the gate by the sign and down an incline to a path at the bottom of the slope by the river. Carry straight on keeping the river on your left. This path is the old track bed of the Glyn Valley Tramway. Keep on this path passing over the river on an old iron bridge and passing a sewage works on the left. After approximately 0.5 mile (0.8 km) go through a gate onto a lane at Pont y Meibion (GR196351).

3 Turn left and continue up the lane which goes round to the right and through a gate at which point the tarmac ends. Continue up the track and over a cattle grid. Bear left at the second 'Y' junction and continue to climb. *Approximately 0.33 mile (0.53 km) after the 'Y' junction sit a while*

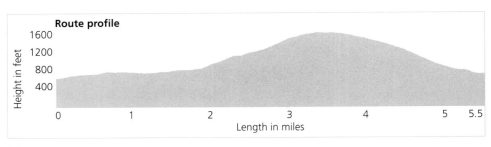

Route profile

Height in feet: 1600, 1200, 800, 400

Length in miles: 0, 1, 2, 3, 4, 5, 5.5

on the seat on the left and enjoy the view.
Continue up the track and through a gate
then bear left to go through another gate
and onto a lane (GR 211345).

4 Turn left and follow the lane past
Springhill Pony Trekking Centre on
the right. Continue along the lane passing a
lane on the right to Pant Farm
(GR 205365).

5 At this point continue down the
lane and turn left at the bottom at
a T junction to return to Glyn Ceiriog.
Alternatively, the walk can be extended
by approximately 2 miles (3.2 km) by
continuing with Walk 5 from point 2.

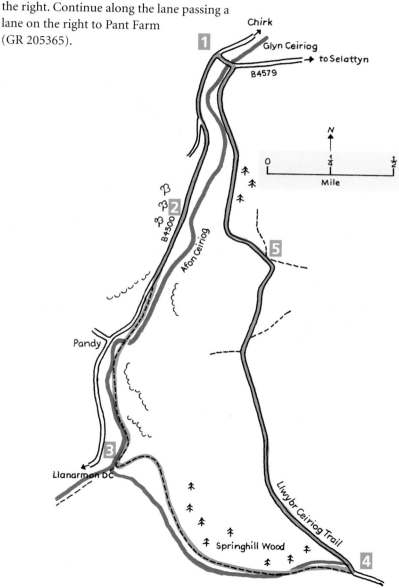

Overton Circuit

Alison Parker

GRADE	Leisurely
MAP	OS Explorer™ Sheets 256 & 257
START POINT	Overton; car park off School Lane, behind St Mary's Church – Grid Ref SJ 374418
DISTANCE	5.6 miles (9.0 km)
TOTAL ASCENT	550 ft (167 m) approx
DURATION	3.0 hours
TERRAIN	Riverside, woods, tracks and lanes. There are magnificent views from Overton towards Llangollen and the Welsh hills

Warning – DO NOT attempt this walk if the River Dee is in flood.

Overton-on-Dee, locally known as Overton, was formally part of Flintshire but is now part of the borough of Wrexham and is about 8 miles from Oswestry.

The churchyard of St Mary the Virgin (at the start/end of the walk) contains a number of very ancient yew trees and is one of the Seven Wonders of Wales. The earliest part of the church is possibly of Norman construction, so the yew trees at 1500-2000 years old predate the church. In 1992 Overton celebrated the 700th anniversary of the granting of a Royal Charter to Overton by Edward I in 1292 with a royal visit from the present queen who planted a new yew tree. Most of the town was once owned by the Bryn-y-pys estate, and in the nineteenth century the owner wielded considerable political influence, as being the landlord of most of the surrounding property was virtually guaranteed of a place in Parliament.

The 'Cocoa and Reading Rooms' (now the library), a terracotta building of 1890 located on the main road just off the end of School Lane is an interesting building. It was built to promote temperance. Other constructions of interest are the alms houses and a Victorian village pump.

This walk takes in part of the Maelor Way, a long-distance footpath which passes through Overton. There is a picnic area adjacent to the church.

DIRECTIONS

1 Exit from the car park to the left and turn again to the left along the churchyard wall. Turn right along the High Street and cross the junction of Bangor Road. Go past the Roman Catholic Church and the recreation ground. Look for a fingerpost on the other side of the road. Take care in crossing the road (GR 369421).

2 Go through the gate. *Looking right there is a lych-gate leading to a small cemetery and the preserved remains of the Chapel, which is part of the Bryn-y-pys estate.* Return to the path and continue

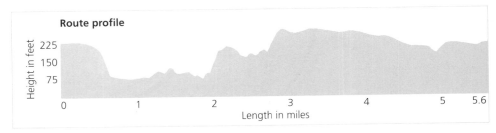

Route profile

Height in feet: 225, 150, 75

Length in miles: 0, 1, 2, 3, 4, 5, 5.6

down the hill following the marked path. Cross the footbridge and bear left following the line of the fence to your left. *You are now walking along the flood plain of the River Dee, locally known as 'the Bottoms', and following the Maelor Way.* Keep close to the river toward some woodland. Looking to the left you may see Overton village overlooking the river plain (GR 362412).

3 Cross the plank bridge into the woods to your right and ignore paths to the left. In wet weather this path can be very muddy and slippery. Continue into a field of rough pasture before more woodland, which in the spring is full of wild garlic. While still following the river the path wriggles its way up and down the hills with several small plank bridges crossing small streams. *On the other side of the river you will shortly see the church at Erbistock and soon after, the Boat Inn. Within a few metres look carefully down the bank to see the* remains of the once landing place of the ferry (GR 356413).

4 The path continues up and down and side to side as it nears the junction of Shell Brook with the edge. Do not follow the path down the long staircase leading to the recently installed bridge over Shell Brook, which has replaced a series of wooden bridges which were regularly washed away when the Dee flooded. Instead leave the Maelor Way and take the path on the left just before the staircase (GR 351411).

5 Walk along the footpath now following the Shell Brook until it reaches the road at Bartons bank. Turn left. With care, in single file walk left up the hill keeping left passing the drive to Knolton Hall and ignore the footpath waymarked on the left. Where a track appears on the left, look for

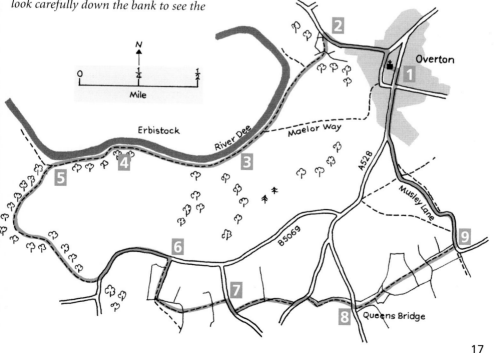

a waymark on the right, nearly opposite, and cross the road with care to a footpath which skirts the edge of a cottage garden (GR 359405).

6 The path leads to a paddock where there is an electric fence on the right of the path. Look for a path ahead which is secreted behind some bushes. Go over the stile and turn left along the field edge. Turn right at the field corner and cross the stile on the left. Walk ahead through two fields to a lane (GR 363402).

7 Go right for a short distance and over the stile on the left to a field edge path to another stile and walk ahead to exit onto another lane. Turn left and after a short distance look out for two gates on the right. Go through the first gate where there is a waymarker on the left-hand post. Walk with the hedge to the left and go through

second gateway. Continue with the hedge on the left to meet the main road (A528) (GR 371402).

8 Turn right and then immediately left across the road to a hard track leading to Queens Bridge. Follow the track and at the right-hand bend bear left by the telegraph pole, through some trees and after crossing the stile bear left and head for a gateway. Go straight on through the field to a stile to the left of a power line post. Cross the stile and bear left to a gate and track. Go over the stile immediately on your right and turn left. Follow the hedgerow to the corner of the field and over the stile to exit abruptly into Musley Lane (GR378406).

9 Go left and follow the lane to return to the main road. Turn right to return to Overton village and the car park.

Queens Head and Montgomery Canal

Pat La-Garde

8

GRADE	Leisurely
MAP	OS Explorer™ Sheet 240
START POINT	Car park opposite the Queens Head Public House – Grid Ref SJ 339268
DISTANCE	4.25 miles (6.84 km)
TOTAL ASCENT	170 ft (52 m) approx
DURATION	2.25 hours
TERRAIN	Good paths, fields, lanes and canal towpath

Note: In wet weather, parts of this walk can be very muddy and dirty.

This area sandwiched, as it is, between the Montgomery Canal and the Shrewsbury to Wrexham railway line is characterised by farms, small villages and hamlets. It is a quiet area to get away from the rush and turmoil of modern life.

The Montgomery Canal has been unused and derelict for many years but is now being restored for cruising with around half of its 35 miles now in water. Starting from its junction with the Llangollen Canal at Welsh Frankton, it meanders through the Welsh Marches to Newtown. The section from Welsh Frankton to Maesbury Marsh is fully restored and open to cruising.

The canal is a true haven for wildlife and tranquillity with a number of Sites of Special Scientific Interest (SSSI) along the way.

DIRECTIONS

1 From the car park turn left and go 50 m along the road then take a road on the right for approximately 100 m to a stile in the right hand hedge. Go diagonally left across the field to a stile in the corner then diagonally right across this next large field towards a telegraph pole. Continue on to reach a stile in the hedge on to a minor road. Turn left and continue for 50 m, then take the road on the right beside a white cottage, this leads into a green lane further on, continue to the end of the green lane and take a stile by small stream. Keeping the hedge on the left go along the field edge to two further stiles either side of a ditch. Cross the next field slightly right to a stile at the railway embankment (GR 345284).

2 Taking extreme care, cross over the railway line into a small copse, then follow the path through to another stile and proceed along the field edge to a gate and stile. Turn immediately right over the stile on to the canal towpath. Follow the canal path south for approx 1 km until Bridge 74 over the canal with two properties on the right-hand side (GR 351276).

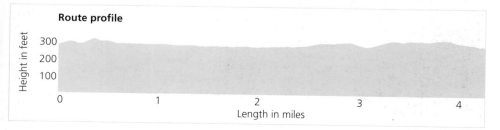

Route profile

Height in feet: 300, 200, 100

Length in miles: 0, 1, 2, 3, 4

19

3 Cross the bridge and road and take a tarmac road straight ahead until reaching Station Farm on the right-hand side. After the end of the buildings take a stile alongside the gate on the right. Keeping the hedge on the right continue to a bridge in the corner of the field. Now go half left across the next field to a stile, then straight on over to the next stile. Cross a small field to a bridge and double gates, again go in a diagonal direction to two stiles in the far left-hand corner. Continue up the next field with the hedge on the left to find a stile in the hedge. From here go slightly left to a stile leading to concrete farm road (GR 349264).

4 Continue straight on for 100 m to a gate and stile in to a farmyard. Turn right up an enclosed farm track. At the junction bear right and then at the white house, go up a small bank on the left to find a small gate and a stile. Cross the field with the hedge on the right to a stile in the corner. Go over and half left heading to a large tree and building at a large gate (this field is often ploughed, just walk across to the gate). Go through the gate onto a lane (GR 345263).

5 Turn right and then follow the lane 350 m down to a junction. Turn right and follow the road back to the Queen's Head.

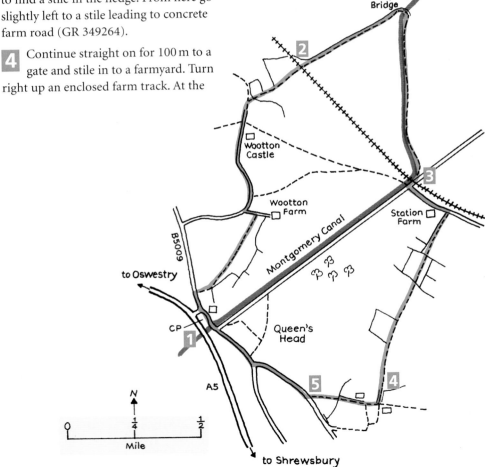

The 'Monty' – Maesbury Marsh, Crickheath and Morton

9

Bob Kimber

GRADE	Leisurely
MAP	OS Explorer™ Sheet 240
START POINT	Canal Central café – Grid Ref SJ 310249. On quiet days, and provided that you have the prior agreement of the owners, you may well be able to park at Canal Central, otherwise, it is a case of finding somewhere safe as near as possible to the start.
DISTANCE	4.6 miles (6.85 km) With optional extension 5.8 miles (8.8 km)
TOTAL ASCENT	120 ft (37 m) approx, with optional extension 160 ft (50 m)
DURATION	2.15 hours
TERRAIN	A canal-side walk, followed by lanes and field paths. The whole of the towpath section of the walk forms part of the Wat's Dyke Way. An optional extension is described after the main route. Very level with few stiles

Note: Parking can be a problem and it is therefore suggested that this walk in not really suitable for large groups.

This walk is partly intended to show how the 'Monty' (or, to give its official name, the Shropshire Union Canal, Montgomeryshire Branch) is gradually being restored to navigation. As you walk westwards, the first part of the canal is fully navigable; then there is a section which is restored but not yet open to traffic. From Redwith Bridge almost to Crickheath Wharf restoration is in progress and thereafter, if you follow the optional extended walk, you can see the canal in its unrestored state. There are some information panels giving historical details about the canal and its use.

DIRECTIONS

1 Access to the canal towpath is either through a gate from the café or via a path dropping down from the lane beside the adjacent bridge over the canal, Bridge 80. Walk westwards along the towpath for 1 ml (1.6 km), passing Crofts Mill Bridge and then walk along the newly restored, but unopened, section to Redwith Bridge (under the B4396) which is Bridge 83 (GR 301241).

2 *To the south is the stark outline of the Breidden Hills and, to the west, the southern end of the Oswestry Uplands from*

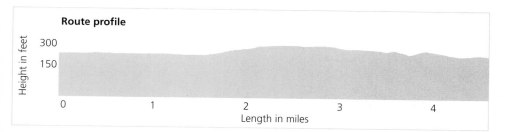

Route profile

Height in feet: 300, 150, 0

Length in miles: 0, 1, 2, 3, 4

Llanymynech Rocks to Sweeney Mountain forms a prominent ridge. In addition to the two lifting bridges, those interested in canals will have noted a couple of 'winding holes' (turning areas), one of which is in use. Continue along the towpath for 0.7 ml (1.1 km), passing the restoration works, until the bridge just before Crickheath Wharf (GR 292235).

3 Leave the towpath and go up the track on the left, through the gate, then turn right and cross over the bridge to take the footpath going westwards through a gap in the hedge directly in front of you. Go through a small area of newly-planted trees and then across the field (where there could be sheep and hens) heading for the new farm buildings – there are two gates in the electric fences. The path comes out to the right of the farm buildings (poultry sheds) through a gate. Cut across the corner of the yard, through another gate and turn right onto the lane (GR 286236).

4 Follow the lane to the crossroads with the B4396 (about 40 m) and go straight over. Care is needed as this is a busy stretch of road. Continue straight ahead through Morton until you reach the next crossroads, about 0.6 m (GR 292246).

5 Turn right down the lane towards Redwith. After 600 m a stile on the left gives access to a short field path across to Morton Farm, there are two more stiles

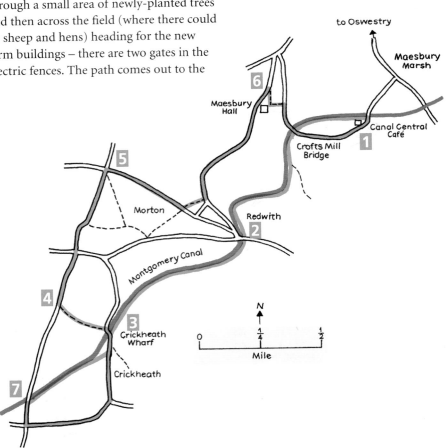

Photo: Old Oswestry Hillfort / Ray Hadlow

at the farm end. Turn left to follow the lane for almost 0.6 ml (1.0 km), passing Maesbury Hall. Shortly after the Hall, turn right into a small industrial estate – Maesbury Mill Industrial Park (GR 303252).

6 The footpath follows the access road towards the buildings and then turns off left alongside a wharf by a boat yard (which is on a private arm of the canal) to join another lane through a gap in the hedge. Turn right onto the lane, continue past the wharf, cross the canal at Croft Mill Bridge and continue straight ahead until you reach a ford. Cross the River Morda via the footbridge and walk along the road to reach Canal Central again (where a well-earned

pot of tea, with a tea cosy, and home-made scone or cake might be on the menu).

Optional extension at Point 3:
Instead of leaving the towpath at (3), continue under the bridge and along the path beside the completely unrestored canal for about 0.75 km to reach a lane at (7) – there are a couple of stiles on this section. Turn left along the lane and take the next turning on the left (signposted: Crickheath). Making sure you don't miss the very interesting old house at East Farm and bearing left at the junction just after the farm, follow this lane for about 0.7 ml (1.15 km) through Crickheath and back to the bridge at (3). Now follow the main walk route from this point.

Bausley Hill and the River Severn

Dawn Milner and Graham Dean

GRADE	Moderate
MAP	OS Explorer™ Sheet 240
START POINT	The layby at Melverley Bridge – Grid Ref SJ 331158
DISTANCE	4.8 miles (7.7 km)
TOTAL ASCENT	670 ft (205 m) approx
DURATION	2.45 hours
TERRAIN	Paths, wood and riverside walk with hill top views, the confluence of the Severn and the Vyrnwy and two pubs

This walk takes you past the confluence of the Severn, the longest river in Great Britain, and one of its tributaries, the Vyrnwy. On Bausley Hill is a Roman encampment, and barrows are scattered about the parish. While in the area it's worth diverting to take a look at the oldest church in Shropshire: St Peter's Church, Melverley. This was founded in 1406 after the chieftain Owain Glyndwr burnt down the wooden chapel on the river bank site in 1401. The church is a timber framed, wattle and daub, black and white construction and is pegged together without a nail in the building.

DIRECTIONS

1 Cross over Melverley Bridge and into Wales, continue along the road to the T junction with the B4393. Cross over the road, turn left and walk for a few metres to a lane just before the Fir Tree pub. Continue up the lane, round a right-hand bend and then a further 300 m to a stile by a metal gate on the left (GR 325153).

2 Go over the stile – Bausley Hill is now ahead. Go straight on and over two stiles to a shallow brook with stiles either side. Cross the stiles and brook, then climb up the steep field ahead to a bridleway waymark on the right at the entrance to a wood (GR 327149).

3 Go through the gate into the wood and turn immediately left to take the track to a grassy area at the top of Bausley Hill. This is marked with a bridleway waymark post, there is also a telephone pole just to the right. Good views here of Rodney's Pillar and place for a coffee break. Now walk diagonally right for a few metres towards Rodney's Pillar to a small un-metalled road. Continue along this road which skirts Kempster's Hill for 0.85 miles (1350 m) until a T junction with a bigger road. Turn right and follow the road for just over 0.33 mile (0.5 km) to a gate on the left. A fingerpost (without the finger) marks this path, there is

Route profile

also a wooden electricity pole in the hedge just ahead left (GR 315144).

4 Walk down the slope to the remnants of a hedge that once edged a track and then up the field to a wooden wicket gate approximately 18 m to the left of the top right-hand corner of the field. Through the gate and turn left to follow the path by the fence at the top of the wood. The path gradually curves down through the wood eventually arriving at a gate into an old scrap yard. Leave the scrap yard by a gate into a lane which leads to the Admiral Rodney pub (GR 311151).

5 Turn right into the road and continue back to Crew Green and the B4396.

Turn right here then in approximately 50 m, take the first lane on the left (Little Belan Lane). Just before the house at the bottom of the lane, at a gate, cross a stile on the left then keep straight ahead from the gate to pass the house just to the right and skirt round the old quarry. Pass through some gated sheep pens (waymarked Severn Way) (GR 319519).

6 Wander down to the river bank. Turn right and follow waymarkers back to the Melverley Bridge. Go under the bridge and turn sharply right to gain the road and cross the bridge to the layby.

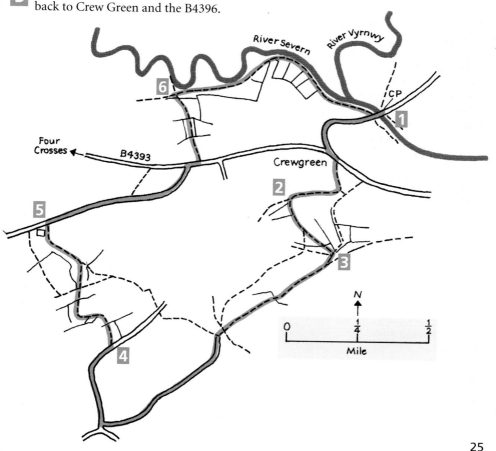

A Stroll around Melverley

Dave Arden

11

GRADE	Leisurely
MAP	OS Explorer™ Sheet 240
START POINT	The layby at Melverley Bridge – Grid Ref SJ 330158
DISTANCE	5.6 miles (9.0 km)
TOTAL ASCENT	136 ft (42 m) approx
DURATION	3 hours
TERRAIN	Field paths, country lane, bridleway

The walk starts by the River Severn but soon follows its tributary, the River Vyrnwy. The bridge over the River Severn was originally a railway bridge, rebuilt in 1948 to carry dolerite from Criggion Quarry and was used until 1959, when it became a road bridge. Melverley Church is an attractive and interesting old building as it is Shropshire's only timber-framed Parish Church, reputed to have been built at the beginning of the fifteenth century. The first part of the walk is along argaes which are raised flood defences as the Severn and Vyrnwy occasionally flood in Winter. Rodney's Pillar is an obelisk on the Breidden Hills dedicated to Admiral Rodney who fought at the Battle of Trafalgar with Lord Nelson. Llanymynech Hill has a spectacular golf course, a Nature Reserve and also two quarries which are part of a restored Limeworks Heritage area at Llanymynech and well worth a visit (see Blodwell Rock and Llanymynech Quarry walk).

DIRECTIONS

1 Cross over the road from the layby and follow the Severn Way along the argae towards Melverley. At the far end of the path turn left, enter the churchyard and immediately turn right and exit through the small wicket gate (GR 333166).

2 The path now goes along the top of the argae to follow the meanders of the River Vyrnwy through gates or over stiles. *From this path there are good views of Rodney's Pillar to the left and Llanymynech Hill and the Berwyns straight ahead. You may also see various water birds, buzzards and perhaps a fox, as well as signs of badgers.* After about 2 miles you will reach a ruin called 'The Shores' (GR 317178).

3 Just before 'The Shores', cross the first stile on the right and go straight across the field towards the elbow of the hedge where there is a clump of large trees. Cross the stile, head diagonally across the field to the gate and stile, then almost immediately turn right through another gate and head for the stile on the left. Cross the next field heading towards two small white posts and the stile located in the middle of the hedge, just behind a clump of bushes. Cross the field to a stile into a lane (GR 322122).

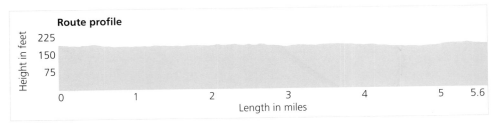

Route profile

Height in feet: 225, 150, 75

Length in miles: 0, 1, 2, 3, 4, 5, 5.6

4 Cross over the lane and the path then go straight through five fields to reach the road (GR 325186).

5 Turn right and follow the road to a stile on the right by a grey bungalow (Glen Vista). Go straight across two fields to reach a road. Turn left and then right to pass Meadow Farm, then a short way further to a wide bridleway on the left (GR 330178).

6 Follow the bridleway, turning left at the bottom and continue to a stile on the right. After crossing this keep close to the left-hand hedge, cross over the

7 Turn right along the road and then almost immediately left down a tarmac lane. A short way down take the stile on the right, marked Severn Way, keeping close to the left-hand hedge and after crossing the next stile, follow the signs over two more stiles and go left diagonally across the last field to reach the road by the Tontine Inn (GR 334166).

8 Go straight ahead towards the Church to pick up the path back to the car park.

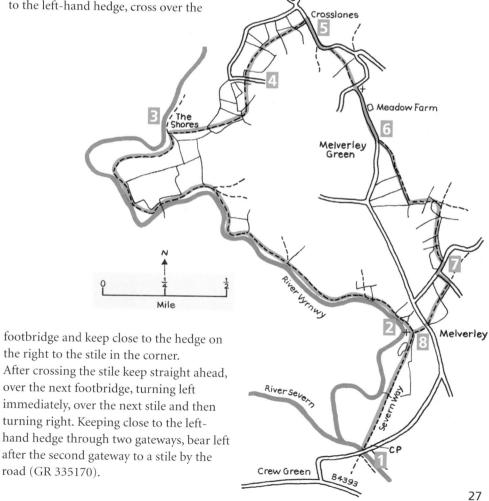

footbridge and keep close to the hedge on the right to the stile in the corner. After crossing the stile keep straight ahead, over the next footbridge, turning left immediately, over the next stile and then turning right. Keeping close to the left-hand hedge through two gateways, bear left after the second gateway to a stile by the road (GR 335170).

27

Blodwel Rock and Llanymynech Quarry

12

Peter Carr

GRADE	Leisurely
MAP	OS Explorer™ Sheet 240
START POINT	Car park at end of Underhill Lane (off the A483 at Pant) and signposted Nature Reserve – Grid Ref SJ 271219
DISTANCE	3.7 miles (5.95 km)
TOTAL ASCENT	690 ft (210 m) approx
DURATION	2.15 hours
TERRAIN	Paths, wood, ridge and quarry walk with extensive views over both the Tanat Valley and the Shropshire Plain

This walk takes in the ridge overlooking the Tanat Valley then circles round to return via Llanymynech Quarry.

Llanymynech has been an important settlement since a hillfort was established in the 10th Century BC. Offa's Dyke passes through the village and mining in the area dates back to Roman times. Most of the industrial remains today are from 19th and 20th century Limeworks. Much of the local rock outcrop on the hill above the village is the result of quarrying over the centuries. Canal and later rail transport allowed limestone quarrying and burning – to produce quicklime – to expand rapidly. The main uses of Llanymynech limestone were in agriculture, building, making iron and steel and possibly lime-based 'paints'. Quarrying ended at Llanymynech in 1914, with Portland cement spelling the end for the lime industry.

Many different orchids can be seen on the quarry site and there is a pair of peregrine falcons that nest on the quarry face. At least 34 species of bird can be found on the heritage site including buzzards, finches, goldcrest, nuthatch, warblers, and woodpeckers.

A diversion from the route during step 6 allows the quarry workings to be explored.

DIRECTIONS

1 Go out of the top of the car park, and in a few metres, just before a gate, go right over a stream to pick up a distinct bridleway. Keep straight on along the path and continue on where the path turns into a private road going past modern houses. At the end of the road turn left and head uphill for approximately 5 minutes (going past a small estate road on the left (The Meadows)) until the road bears right with another road forking left. Take the left fork (but not

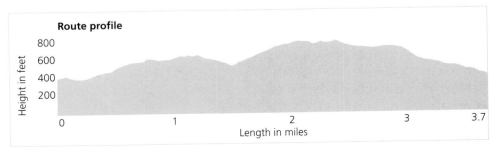

Route profile

Rose Mount Drive, which is sharp left) and continue for 2 minutes until road swings right and Primrose Lane comes in from the left. Take the track straight ahead up to and through the kissing gate (GR 271225).

2 From the kissing gate, turn hard right and take the track through the trees to follow the line of the back gardens to arrive at a stile. Go over the stile and cross the fields diagonally left to a hedge, then turn left and follow the hedge to a field on the right enclosed by a barbed wire fence. Turn right and go through the hedge line and continue up the field with the barbed wire on the left. In 50 m go through another hedge line, then in a further 50 m go through a third hedge line. Continue for another 50 m to a stile. Go over the stile and continue straight on to pick up a muddy farm track, go along the track to a gate and stile. Cross the stile into a lane (GR 272229).

3 Turn right and go down the lane for 100 m and then take the lane on the left (marked with a bridleway fingerpost). Continue along the track for 0.65 km (0.4 ml) to a confluence of lanes by a house on the right. Head diagonally left through the bushes to a gate into a field. Go through the gate and go down the field and then bear left to skirt a fenced pond (there are great crested newts in the pond). Just after the pond turn right and take the left-hand kissing gate into the woods. Go slightly left and follow the waymarked path through

29

the woods (do not go down the bank). At a crossroad of paths, marked with waymarks, turn right and follow the path as it weaves through the woods to come out at some concrete steps – known locally as Jacob's Ladder (GR 270237).

4 Go up the steps and follow a clear path along the top of the bank *(there are a number of lookout points giving marvellous views over the Tanat Valley)* until the path drops down steeply for a short distance into a dip to join Offa's Dyke Path (signposted with a fingerpost with an acorn on it) coming in from the right (GR 266227).

5 Go straight on up the other side of the dip to follow the Offa's Dyke Path to come out on the edge of Llanymynech golf course. Turn right and continue to follow the Offa's Dyke Path skirting round the edge of the golf course. After 150 m,

re-enter the woods and continue on the Offa's Dyke Path to come out at the top end of the golf course (GR 261219).

6 Go ahead 75 m round the edge of the golf course and then turn right to go though a gate to follow the Offa's Dyke Path down though the woods. At the kissing gates (Wales/England border) go through and straight on to pass a restored winding house and some of the quarry workings. *There are wild orchids in the grass below the quarry face and peregrine falcons nest on the quarry wall.* The path passes along the top of some abandoned lime kilns on the right. (50 m past the kilns there is a path back to the right that allows the bottom of the kilns to be viewed.) Continue past the top of the path to the kilns to return to the gate at the start of the walk.

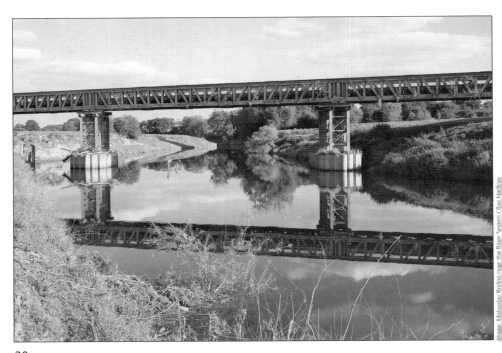

Photos: Melverley Bridge over the River Severn / Ray Hadlow

Llanarmon Mynydd Mawr

Peter Carr

GRADE	Moderate
MAP	OS Explorer™ Sheet 255
START POINT	Llanrhaeadr Ym Mochnant – car parking area across and just up from the Hand public house – Grid Ref SJ 125261
DISTANCE	5.5 miles (8.85 km)
TOTAL ASCENT	1330 ft (406 m) approx
DURATION	3.5 hours
TERRAIN	Good paths, fields, lanes and rough tracks. A long ascent followed by a descent and then lanes

This walk leaves from Llanrhaeadr on the waterfall road and very quickly takes to the hills to the north to circle round to Llanarmon Mynydd Mawr and St Garmon's Church, before returning to Llanrhaeadr via tracks, moorland and fields.

The highlight of this walk is undoubtedly the small church of St Garmon's at Llanarmon Mynydd Mawr. Nestling among trees in its quiet and remote location with a backdrop of hills, it is a place to sit and contemplate the surrounding views of the Tanat Valley, the circling buzzards (and if you are lucky, the red kites), and in spring the gambolling lambs. The Church is thought to be of early medieval origin, but was 'restored' to a 19th century design by W.H Spaull of Oswestry in 1886. The church is still in use serving the scattered and sparsely populated community with services twice a month.

1st Sunday in the month – 11.15 am Morning Prayer

3rd Sunday in the month – 11.15am Holy Communion

All are welcome.

The church is normally open, but if not, the key can be obtained from the address advertised in the church porch. If you visit, please leave a donation in the collecting box.

DIRECTIONS

1 From the car park, head down the road past the Hand public house and in a few metres, turn right up a small road past the old school to intersect with the road to the waterfall. Turn right and continue on the road for approximately 3 minutes to the steep uphill driveway to Arllwyn on your right (there is a fingerpost in the hedge on the left marking the driveway as a public footpath). Go up the drive and through the gate into the woods, then continue on up the path through the wood to the stile at the top (GR 122265).

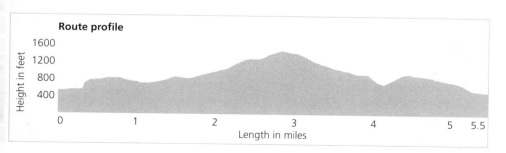

Route profile

Height in feet: 1600, 1200, 800, 400

Length in miles: 0, 1, 2, 3, 4, 5, 5.5

2 Go over the stile and head slightly diagonally left over the rise in the field, then as you cross the rise, head for the stile just to the right of the gate. Cross the stile and in approx 10 m cross a second stile into another field. Head up the field with the hedge on your left to the top of the field (Hen Fache farm is to the right). Take the gate on the left and continue to head up the field, now with the hedge on the right, to a stile onto a road (GR 124271).

3 Cross the stile (steep descent onto the road), cross the road diagonally left to go over another stile up a steep bank into a field. Go down the field with the hedge on your right and at the bottom of the field, turn left and continue along the field boundary to a stile in the corner. Cross the stile and head steeply down the field with the trees on your left. At the bottom of the field head left into the trees to a substantial footbridge over the stream (GR 127275).

4 Go over the footbridge and up the field with the fence on the right for approximately 50 m. Take the stile on the right and immediately cross the small stream. Head diagonally left up the field to a stile in the top corner of the field. Cross the stile and another small stream, then with the hedge on the left continue along the field edge to a gate. Go over the stile and continue along the field edge to another gate ahead. Go through the gate and follow a farm track up to a gate onto a tarmac lane. Turn right and go along the lane to a T junction. Turn left and continue ahead going slightly up hill for approximately 0.5 km to a T junction. Take the left turn and continue for a few metres to the church (St Garmon's) (GR 135279).

The church is normally open and is worth a visit – see notes above.

5 From the church, continue to the gate ahead marked with a bridleway sign and go up the field keeping the rough boggy area just to your left to reach an informal stile (note that the official footpath is along the boggy area, but this is virtually unusable). Cross the stile and continue up the field with the track in a dip just below. When the terrain permits, regain the track and continue uphill to a metal gate onto a moorland track. Keep on the track as it circles round the hill (to the right) to another gate. Go through the gate and keep along the track until you reach a metal feed cage. Continue for a few more metres to a fence and turn left and go 20 m down to a gate. Do NOT go through the gate, turn left onto a bridleway and continue downhill for 20 m to intersect a substantial lane (GR 125288).

6 Turn left onto the lane and go down hill for approximately 10 minutes to a gate with a small abandoned quarry on the left. Go through the gate and continue downhill for approximately a further 10 minutes to another gate by a small barn (converted to a dwelling) (GR 128279).

7 Go through the gate and after a few metres, take the stile on the right. Head diagonally left down the field and go through the hedge line to continue diagonally left downhill to reach the substantial bridge crossed at step 4. Go over the bridge and then go right, over a stile and then immediately left to cross a second stile. Go steeply uphill, diagonally right to a stile at the top. Cross the stile and skirt the edge of the field round to the right for a short way and then head across the field to a stile in the hedge. Go straight ahead across the field to a line of trees and then head diagonally right to a stile just ahead of a drive to a house (GR 123275).

8 Cross the stile onto a tarmac lane and turn left. Go along the lane for approximately 250 m to a junction, then take the lane on the right. Go along the lane for approximately 300 m

to a stile on the left (just before a bend in the lane with farm buildings ahead right). Go over the stile and keeping the fence/hedge to the right, go down through three fields (crossing two stiles) to arrive at a stile on the right into woods (point 2 on the outward leg of the walk). Go down the track through the woods reversing the outward route to the waterfall road. Turn left and go along the road to return to the start of the walk.

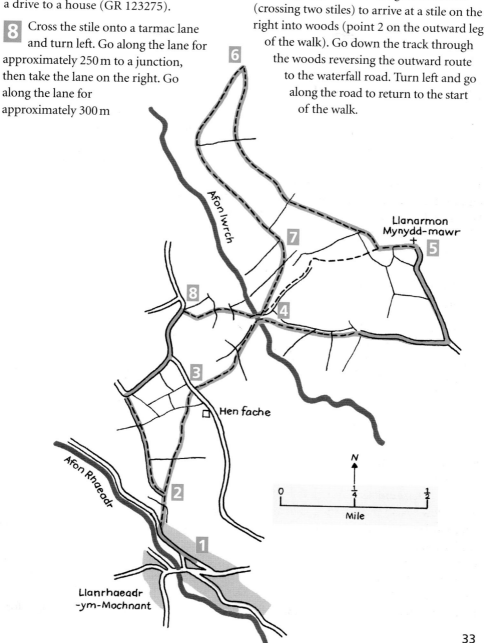

N

0   1/4   1/2

Mile

Moel Hen-fache circuit

Peter Carr

14

GRADE	Moderate
MAP	OS Explorer™ Sheet 255
START POINT	Llanrhaeadr Ym Mochnant – car parking area across and just up from the Hand public house – Grid Ref SJ 125261
DISTANCE	5.9 miles (9.49 km)
TOTAL ASCENT	1275 ft (389 m) approx
DURATION	3.5 hours
TERRAIN	Good paths, fields, lanes, access land (moorland) and rough tracks. A long ascent followed by a descent and then lanes

This walk leaves from Llanrhaeadr on the waterfall road and then does a circuit of Moel Hen-fache taking in access land at the top. The walk affords wonderful views of the Tanat Valley and the Berwyn Mountains

Note: It is advised that this walk should not be undertaken if visibility is poor or the weather is bad as it takes in exposed open moorland where navigation can be difficult.

This walk starts from the picturesque village of Llanrhaeadr Ym Mochnant in the heart of the Tanat Valley. Whilst essentially agricultural, the village attracts many visitors, being the gateway to Pistyll Rhaeadr, the highest waterfall in Wales (3 miles from the village). The waters of the River Disgynfa cascade 240 ft down a mossy tree-flanked cliff and through a natural arch into a deep pool. There is a tea room below the waterfall where one can sit and enjoy the spectacular falls while partaking of refreshments.

St Dognan's Church is in the centre of the village and is where, in the 16th century, the Reverend William Morgan completed the first translation of the Bible into Welsh and in so doing did much to ensure the survival of the language. William Morgan later went on to become Bishop of Llandaff and the Bishop of St Asaph. The church itself has had many changes and additions, the oldest part dating from the 13th century, is the nave and the north transept, the south transept was added in the 14th century. The lower section of the tower is believed to be Augustinian, with the upper section dating to the 18th century. The north porch and vestry were added in the 19th century.

In 1995, Llanraeadr was the location for the film 'An Englishman Who Went Up A Hill But Came Down A Mountain' starring Hugh Grant. The Plough Inn was one of the main locations and today is a busy local pub offering meals and B&B.

DIRECTIONS

1 From the car park, head down the road passing the Hand public house and in a few metres, turn right up a small

Route profile

road past the old school to intersect with the road to the waterfall. Turn right and continue on the road for approximately 3 minutes to the steep uphill driveway to Arllwyn on your right (there is a fingerpost in the hedge on the left marking the drive way as a public footpath). Go up the drive and through the gate into the woods, then continue on up the path through the wood to the stile at the top (GR 122265).

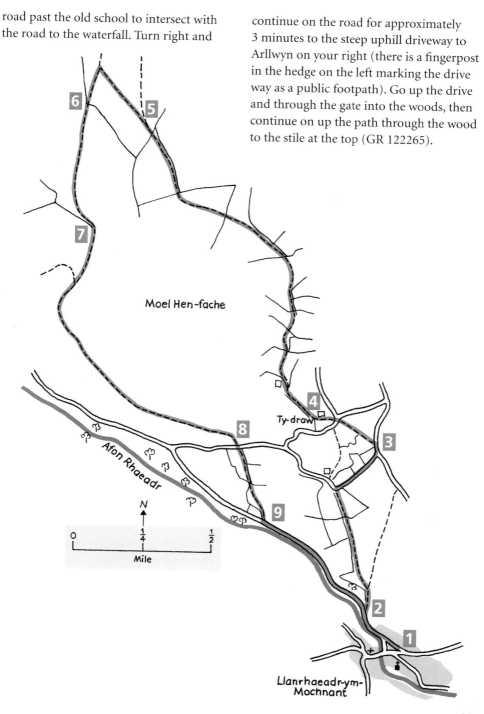

Moel Hen-fache

Afon Rhaeadr

Ty-draw

N

0   1/4   1/2
Mile

Llanrhaeadr-ym-Mochnant

2 Go over the stile and turn left, keeping the hedge on the left, cross three fields and three stiles to exit onto a lane opposite farm buildings. Turn right and go along the lane for 5 minutes to a T Junction, turn left and continue for 50 m to a path and stile through the hedge on the left (GR 122274). (This may be slightly obscured by vegetation – look for the drain grid on the left of the lane and the path is just by it).

3 Go over the stile and follow the hedge round to the right to go through a gate (at the time of writing, this was very dilapidated and laying back against the hedge). Cross the field heading for a gate ahead and exit onto a lane. Turn right and after a few metres turn left up a driveway to Ty-Draw (there is a fingerpost marking this as a right of way). Follow the waymarks through the grounds of Ty-Draw, keeping the house to the right, to arrive at a stile (GR 119275).

4 Go over the stile and turn right to follow the hedge (hedge on right), cross another stile and continue to follow the hedge to reach a farm on the right. Go through the gate on the right immediately past the farm buildings, then immediately go left through another gate. Turn right and follow the hedge (hedge on the right) to a gate which exits onto a broad track. Keep on the track for 0.75 miles (1.21 km), crossing stiles and going through a number of gates on the way until you see a wood just ahead and to the right where you will find a gateway (no gate) with a waymarker on the right-hand post. Go through the gateway and keep the fence on your right to reach a stile. Cross the stile and go along the field edge with a wood on

the right and go past sheep pens to reach a gate with an Access Land marker on the left-hand post (GR 109295).

5 Go through the gate and follow the broad track for approximately 10 minutes to a small bridlewaymarker located to the left of the track. (If you go past a small and old quarry, you have gone too far, the bridleway is about 200 m before this). Take the bridleway across the moor heading approximately south until the fence that comes in from the right intersects with a fence ahead at a gate in the corner (GR 106286).

6 Go through the gate and follow the faint bridleway over the moor, trending left and gradually downhill until you see a fence ahead and a fence coming in from the left with a gate in the corner. Head for the gate (GR 105283).

7 Go through the gate onto a broad but rough track and continue for 1.2 miles (1.93 km) to intersect a road (GR 114273).

8 At the road turn left, then almost immediately take the stile on the right (marked with a fingerpost). Go down the field with the fence to your left to a gate at the bottom of the field. Go through the gate and down the field now with the hedge on your right, continue round the field boundary to a stile in the bottom left-hand corner of the field. Cross the stile and then a small footbridge and go down the field with the hedge to the right to a stile at the bottom (GR 116287).

9 Cross the stile onto the road (the road to the waterfall) and turn left to follow the road back to Llanrhaeadr and the start of the walk.

Llangedwyn and Briw

Pat La-Garde

GRADE	Moderate
MAP	OS Explorer™ Sheet 239
START POINT	Car park next to Llangedwyn Mill (Craft Centre) – Grid Ref SJ 185241
DISTANCE	5.4 miles (8.7 km)
TOTAL ASCENT	990 ft (302 m) approx
DURATION	3.25 hours
TERRAIN	Good paths, fields and woods

This walk leaves Llangedwyn and goes over fields to Llangedwyn Hall then up through woods and tracks to the small hamlet of Briw and then returns via lanes and fields to Llangedwyn.

There are spectacular views of the Tanat Valley and the Berwyn mountains.

The walk starts from Llangedwyn Mill, a group of buildings beside the Afon Tanat which were formerly a pub, shop, mill and farm and have now been converted into a craft centre and a post office by the Antur Tanat Cain charity.

The small parish of Llangedwyn centres on the Williams-Wynn estate of Llangedwyn Hall, a listed building which has an important 18th century formal terraced garden. The gardens are occasionally open to the public via the National Garden Scheme (Yellow Book).

DIRECTIONS

1 Leave the car park at Llangedwyn Mill and go right on the road for a few metres. Look for gate in the hedge near the bridge and take the path diagonally left (the fingerpost points wrongly, head directly towards Llangedwyn Hall) through a gate and across another field to Llangedwyn village. Cross the road and take the driveway just right of the bus shelter leading to the rear of Llangedwyn Hall. Turn right behind the stable block and up an incline for 100 m, then turn left into woodland and follow the bridleway (there are a number of small jumps which are easy to get over) to the end of the woodland. Go through a dilapidated gate and straight across the field to join a well defined path going left into woodland (GR 193251).

2 Stay on the path and bear right at the junction, then go up the hill to another path and bear left. Continue to where this path turns left to go straight over the stile in the fence and keeping the hedge or fence on your right, go across the field to an opening in the hedge and a stream. Continue up the field to large gate in the far corner

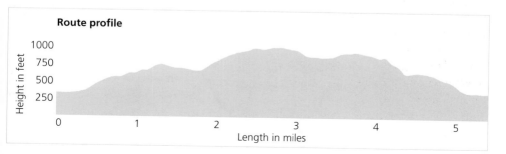

Route profile

Height in feet / Length in miles

and almost immediately another gate on your left. Now head up to a gate into the farmyard. Go through the farmyard to exit onto a minor road (GR 178257). *Note that occasionally there is a bull in the field just below the farm, in these circumstances the farmer has no objection to a route being taken below the farm (a field below where the bull is) to exit via a gate onto the road below the farm buildings.*

3 Turn right onto the road and after 200 m turn left onto another road that will become a track leading to a gate and WOW!!!! the whole of the Berwyn Range is in front of you. After taking pictures, walk on following the hedge on your right to a gate and on to pass a water trough. Turn right again and head through another gate on the skyline. Now go straight across the field to a gate and track, passing a property on the left-hand side. This will meet a minor road and the small hamlet of Briw – continue on to the crossroad (GR 178265).

4 Go straight over and, on passing a lake on the right, in 1.5 km turn right onto a track at the end of a double bend in the road. Follow this track into woodland and after a short distance turn right onto a path and follow it downhill (GR 185254).

5 Descend to a larger track and a renovated cottage on the right. Cross a small stream and look for a gate on the left into a field. Keeping the hedge on the right continue along to a farm gate into a paddock. Go ahead through the paddock, passing a farm (Pen-y-bryn) and down the farm drive to reach the road. Turn left going downhill back to Llangedywn, cross the road and return to the start over the footpath (used on the outward leg) opposite.

N

0   ¼   ½
Mile

Mynydd-y-briw

Pen-y-bryn

to Llanrhaeadr-ym-Monchant

Llangedwyn

Llangedwyn Hall

Craft Centre

CP

B4396

to Oswestry

Afon Tanat

39

Trefonen to Craig Sychtyn Nature reserve and back via the Mynydd Myfyr

16

Helen Hunter-Hayes

GRADE	Moderate
MAP	OS Explorer™ Sheet 240
START POINT	Chapel Green car park (opposite the church in Trefonen) – Grid Ref SJ 260267
DISTANCE	6.0 miles (9.66 km)
TOTAL ASCENT	997 ft (295 m) approx
DURATION	3 hours
TERRAIN	Lanes, Offa's Dyke Path, field tracks and heath

Warning – in wet weather this walk can be very muddy and slippery.

Trefonen is today a small busy country village located approximately 3 miles from Oswestry. There is a pub – the Barley Mow and a shop. There are records that showed the village existed in 1272. The current village largely owes its existence to the mineral works in the 18th and 19th centuries with the mining of coal and the quarrying of limestone and associated pottery and brickworks. When mineral extraction ceased, Trefonen returned once again to its traditional rural roots of farming.

The Offa's Dyke earthwork ran through the village and it is still visible today, in small sections, running adjacent to Chapel Lane. The walk follows part of the Offa's Dyke Path which runs through the village and traces the route of the Dyke.

The walk also passes through Craig Sychtyn Nature Reserve, a carboniferous limestone rock. Wildlife includes green woodpecker, great spotted woodpecker, buzzards, and rare plants include the stinking iris (roast beef plant) and the nettle-leaved bellflower.

DIRECTIONS

1 Leave the car park and pass the Barley Mow, turn right into Bellan Lane, passing the village shop/post office on the left, until the lane bends to the right. At this point leave Bellan Lane and carry on straight ahead along a track, over a stile and into a field (GR 257266).

2 You are now on the Offa's Dyke Path (marked with the sign of an acorn). Go straight on with the hedge on the right and cross another stile. Bear slightly left and go over the stone slab bridge over Trefonen Brook (it may be muddy), and then over the next stile. Continue to follow the Offa's Dyke Path straight ahead, going uphill with an old hollow way on the left. You

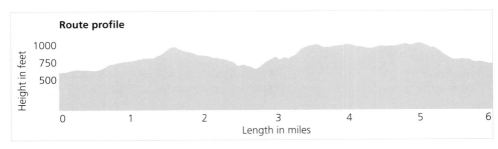

Route profile

Height in feet / Length in miles

40

will pass two large trees, one of which is a small-leaved lime, which is indigenous to the Welsh border area. Continue to the next stile and cross into a lane (GR 250262).

3 Still following Offa's Dyke Path, leave the stile, turn left and then almost immediately right to Canol farm and continue on through the farmyard and through the gate along the track. Take the stile on the right and continue uphill with the hedge on the right. At the marker post, turn left and follow the track up to the stile, cross it and turn right. Continue to follow the Offa's Dyke signs to the top of the Moelydd (GR245253).

4 *From the top there are wonderful views of Shropshire and the Welsh mountains.* Head south-east (140°), downhill to re-join

the Offa's Dyke Path after about 100 m, go between two large gateposts to join a wider path. At this point the Offa's Dyke Path turns left, but our route continues straight on downhill, with a hedge on the left. The path soon broadens out onto a large track. Continue until you reach a corner of this field, ignore the stile off to the left and turn sharp right and continue along this lower path with the hedge on the left. At the end of this hedge you will come to a stile, with another stile ahead over a sunken track – cross both stiles. Now head slightly left and head for a small metal gate by an old tree. Take care as this crossing can be very wet. Continue ahead with the hedge of this next field on your left and pass the white house (Bronynant). Take the stile just past the house and head for the road (GR 240256).

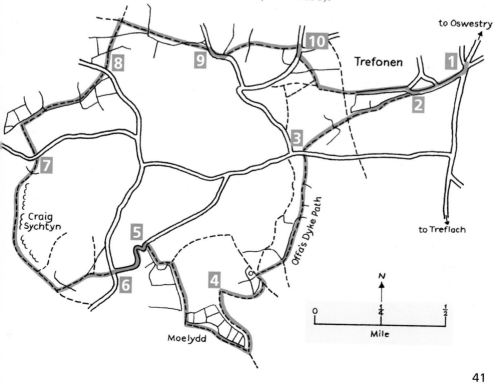

5 At the road, turn left and walk downhill, through a ford and then up hill to a T junction. Take care on this road as the surface can be slippery in wet and cold weather (GR 238255).

6 At the T junction, ahead you will see some steps leading to a stile; cross the stile and keeping the hedge on your right, continue up the hill until you reach an old tree. Where the field boundary bears off to the right, continue left passing an old oak tree, then continue ahead on this path, which is signposted into the woods. You will see a stile ahead – cross this stile and enter the woods heading downhill on a visible trail. You will then reach another trail – turn right and continue uphill on this larger path to reach a triangular patch, with a few very tall trees. Take the path on the right heading for a wooden gate into the Craig Sychtyn Nature Reserve. Continue along the path, through the reserve, keeping the fence on the left and at the end of the Reserve enter a lane, turn right and continue along the path for about 280 m to a stone slab with a metal rail over this. Cross this into the field, and continue ahead to a stile by the gate. Cross the stile into a small lane (GR 233262). *Along this lane is a disused lime kiln, with a second one in front of the quarry in the next field.*

7 Turn left and almost immediately find a stile in the right-hand hedge. Cross this stile, turn right and walk north-west in front of some trees. At a clearing of the coppice continue to the next coppice north, heading for a metal gate to the right of a stone cottage. At the gate, do not go through the gate, but turn right and continue up the field with the hedge to the left to another metal gate in the corner of the field. Take the path straight ahead; you now have excellent views of the Mynydd Myfyr. Keeping the hedge to the right cross the next stile into another field. Bear slightly left and continue ahead, aiming for the left of a field boundary visible ahead. You will now see the stile ahead. Cross and enter onto a road (GR 238267).

8 Cross the road, and cross the stile into the field ahead, bear left, cross a plank bridge prior to crossing the stile. Now go slightly right to a stile in a hedge, continue to the next stile in a hedge but do not cross this stile, but instead turn right and cross a stile and stone slab over a stream. Climb up the bank and continue straight ahead. The next stile in located in trees at the top right corner of the field. Cross the stile into a coppice (take care as this path can be wet), over a second stile and out into another field. Head slightly right, half way up the hedge to another stile, cross this and bear left heading to a gate and stile onto a lane (GR 244269).

9 Turn right and walk along the lane a short way to reach a stile on the left, take this into a field, and head for the farm track ahead. Turn left and continue on this track, through New Barns farmyard onto a road (GR 250269).

10 Turn right and after 50 m take a bridle path on the left, down between two hedges. At the bottom, turn left. This lane becomes Little London Road and at the end of this road, turn right into Bellan Lane. Walk along this road, passing where your track turned off earlier (point 2), and re-trace your steps back to the start.